PAPER
MAGIC

Animals
and Birds

DRAGON'S WORLD

CHILDREN'S BOOKS

Dragon's World Ltd
Limpsfield
Surrey RH8 0DY
Great Britain

First published by Dragon's World 1995

Text: Florence Temko
Editor: Kyla Barber
Design: Mel Raymond, Bob Scott
Illustrations: John Walls
Art Director: John Strange
Editorial Director: Pippa Rubinstein

**The catalogue record for this book is
available from the British Library**

ISBN 1 85028 372 9

Printed in Italy

CONTENTS

PAPERS TO USE

Paper

You use paper every day. Just think of the many kinds you see in school, at home and in shops. They can all be turned into paper animals.

At the beginning of each project you'll find a suggestion for the best paper to use for that animal.

You can substitute other papers and perhaps create something you never expected.

Card

Card or cardboard is stiffer and heavier than paper.

It comes in many thicknesses and weights. Index cards are suitable for small projects. Card, cereal boxes and posterboard are better for larger animals that stand up.

Reuse, recycle

Before you throw away any papers, think about whether you could turn them into an animal. As you make some of the things shown in this book you will be cutting up a lot of paper. You can easily recycle all those funny shapes that fall off.

Turn them into stickers that you glue on to other projects.

Glue

You can use your favourite glue, but always spread on as little as possible. Otherwise the paper may buckle.

My favourite glues are white glue and glue sticks (they must be fresh).

With some glue the paper sticks, but can be lifted off again so that you can rearrange a design until you like it best.

Coatings

Paper animals can be coated to make them last longer. PVC (white glue), lightly spread, will dry clear. Test other acrylic finishes on scraps of paper before applying them.

Measurements

All dimensions are given in centimetres and inches. They are not always exactly equal to avoid too many fractions. Either set will work well.

ANYTHING GOES

This book shows how to make animals using all kinds of paper techniques. Create animals different from those shown using the same techniques. For example, the African animals on page 17 are made with the slit-slit method. You could make a wolf, a penguin or an elephant in the same way.

Add-ons

Have fun adding all kinds of confetti, ribbons, paper cutouts, seeds, snipped-up pieces of colourful paper, feathers.

Colour

In nature animals may be camouflaged for their safety, like jungle tigers. Or they may flaunt a brilliant tail for showing off, like the peacock.

Fortunately when you make paper animals and birds you can colour them close to their natural markings or in any crazy way you like.

Anything goes!

KEY TO SYMBOLS

Crease paper up (valley fold)

- - - - - - - - - - - - - -

A crease made before

_____

Turn the paper over from back to front

Arrow points in the direction in which the paper is to be folded

Double arrow means fold and then unfold the crease.

Cut

FISH BONES

A storm threw the fish on a rock and now only the skeleton is left.

You will need
*A piece of paper
Pencil, scissors*

1 Fold the paper in half.

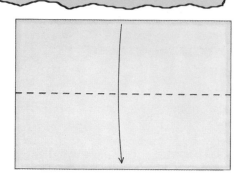

5 Unfold the paper carefully and s–t–r–e–t–c–h it.

2 Draw on half a fish. Cut it out.

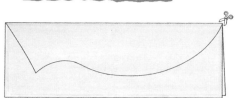

4 Make parallel cuts in between the ones you have just made, but not all the way across. Make some cuts on the tail.

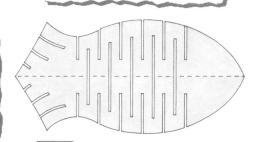

6 Fish Bones.

3 Make parallel cuts beginning at the curved edge, but do not cut all the way across.

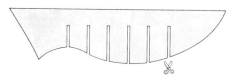

Mobile
Make several Fish Bone skeletons and hang them as a mobile.

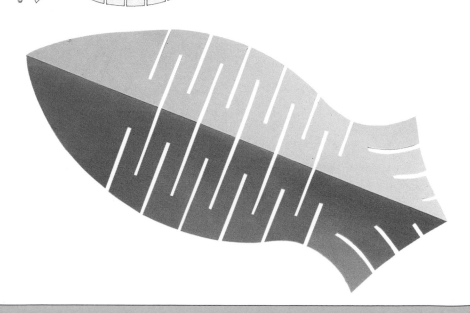

CAMEL

Cut out a camel and pleat it; it stands up. You can decide whether it lives in the zoo or the desert. It depends whether you cut out fences or sand dunes around it.

1 Fan pleat a piece of paper with creases 2 cm (1 in) apart.

2 Stretch the paper flat. Draw on a camel, showing all four legs. Cut it out. Pleat it loosely to make it stand.

3 Camel.

More animals

Make other pleated animals to live with the camel. How about a dromedary?

Do you know how it's different from a camel?

A dromedary has only one bump, but a camel has two.

ORIGAMI BIRD

You only need a square of paper to make an origami bird. Several of them make wonderful table decorations.

You will need
A paper square with sides between 15 and 20 cm (6 in to 9 in)

1 Fold the square corner to corner.

2 Fold the triangle in half.

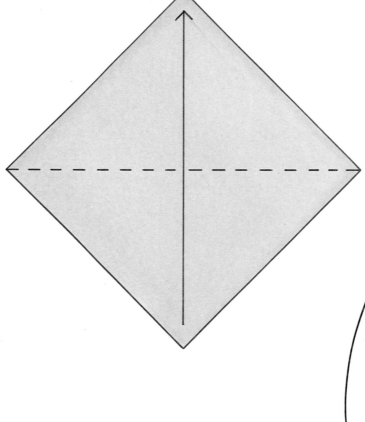

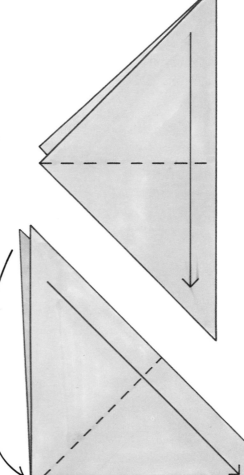

3 Fold the front flap over, as shown by the dotted line. Turn the paper over and fold the back flap in the same way.

4 Make the wings: fold the front flap to stick out over the longer edge. Turn the paper over and fold the back flap in the same way.

5 Pull the beak down in between the two layers of paper. Crease it to make it stay in place. Fold up the feet on the front and the back.

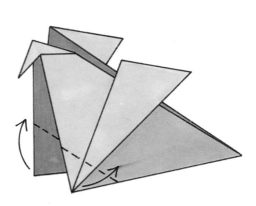

6 Origami Bird.

KITCHEN FOIL SWAN

Wrap kitchen foil around a small ball of crushed paper and shape it into a swan or turkey.

You will need
*Kitchen foil
2 paper tissues*

1 Tear off a good size piece of foil, 50 cm (20 in). Ball up two tissues and place them in the middle of the foil. Bring up the long sides. Overlap them twice into a tight seam.

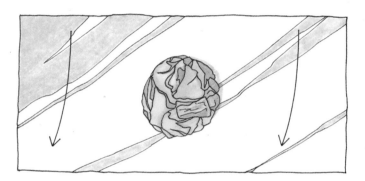

3 Crunch one end together tightly. Shape it into the neck and head of a swan. Spread the other end into the swan's tail feathers. If necessary, carefully tear off any extra at both ends.

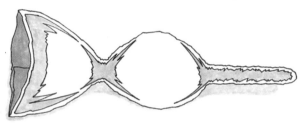

4 Kitchen Foil Swan.

2 Squeeze the foil in two places near the middle with the tissues inside.

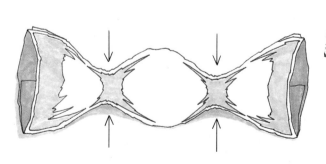

MERMAIDS

Mermaids are fantasy creatures which are half human and half fish. Many stories have been written about them in countries all over the world. You can make a beautiful mermaid with the head, shoulders and arms of a woman and the body and tail of a fish or seal.

1 Place two pieces of paper on top of each other. On the top sheet draw the outline of a mermaid. Draw on the face, hair, fish scales and other features. Cut on the outline, through both layers of paper.

2 Staple around the edges, but leave a large opening on a long edge for stuffing. Tear or cut the scrap paper into strips. Crush and stuff them inside the mermaid.
Be very careful in narrow parts. Staple the stuffing hole closed.

3 Mermaid.
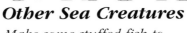

Other Sea Creatures
Make some stuffed fish to keep the mermaid company!

DRAGON CUTOUT

Intricate paper cutting is a popular craft in China and a normal school subject. You can try out this craft by cutting a simple dragon. In the Orient, dragons represent goodness and strength.

You will need
A piece of coloured paper
Tracing paper and pencil or photocopy
Scissors

1 Trace or photocopy the dragon. Place the completed copy on a piece of coloured paper and cut the design through both layers.

Helpful Hints

Here are two ways used by Chinese paper-cutters that will help you cut the dragon.

• *When you cut curves, move the paper and hold the scissors still.*

• *Cut out the eye by making a small slit to the piece you want to remove. The arrow shows where to make a slit. It disappears when you glue the dragon on some background paper.*

2 Dragon Cutout.

Greeting Card

Glue the dragon on a blank greeting card. The illustration shows a very intricate, authentic Chinese cutout. Perhaps you can add some of its features to the simple dragon you have made, or make another, more complex dragon which looks more like this one. Stick the dragon on a piece of background paper.

13

FAVOURITE FROG

It jumps! It's an amphibian! It's one of the best origamis you can make.

You will need
A piece of coloured, heavy paper

1 Make a crease right through the middle of the corner, folding the short edge to the long edge. Unfold the paper, so that it is flat.

2 Fold the other corner at the short edge in the same way. Unfold the paper flat. You now have an X.

3 Crease to the BACK (mountain fold) right through the middle of the X. Unfold the paper.

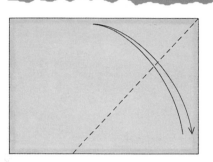

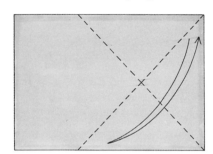

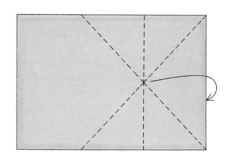

4 Push down at O. Bring up the sides A and B to meet. Then push down and flatten the triangle just formed on the front. See the next drawing.

5 Fold the outer corners of the triangle to the corner.

6 Fold the straight sides to the middle.

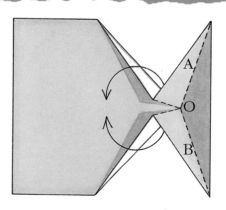

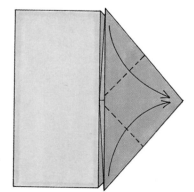

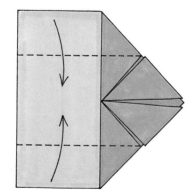

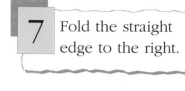

7 Fold the straight edge to the right.

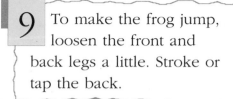

8 Bring the same edge down to the left.

9 To make the frog jump, loosen the front and back legs a little. Stroke or tap the back.

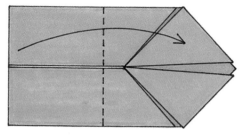

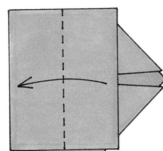

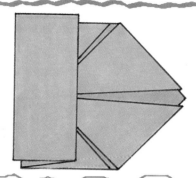

10 Favourite Frog.

In a Pond

Imagine bullfrogs croaking loadly in a lily pond. Create a watery scene by cutting a large piece of blue paper and populate it with frogs. Add white and pink lilies and perhaps butterflies and insects. See if you can get your frogs to jump onto the lily pads, or into a bowl.

Tap here.

LIZARD

Chameleons can change their skin colour for camouflage so that they seem to disappear in their surroundings. Geckos are little lizards that scurry around and like to bask in the sun. Most lizards live in warm, dry climates.

1 Draw, trace or copy the outline of the lizard. Cut it out. Fold the legs as shown. Decorate it any way you like.

2 Lizard.

Other lizards
You can make little and big paper lizards, because they come in all sizes. Iguanas grow up to 1.8 metres (6 ft).

3-D lizards
Make lizards from strong paper or thin card. They will stand up if you bend down the legs and bend up the feet. You can create a desert scene by setting them on a piece of sandpaper or brown paper and adding some cacti cut from green paper.

ZEBRA AND GIRAFFE

Zebras and giraffes live on the African savannah. Zebras use their stripes to confuse hunters. Giraffes use their long necks to reach leaves high up in trees.

1 Draw, trace or photocopy the two pieces. Place the tracing or photocopy on top of the paper.

4 Zebra.

2 Cut out the pieces through both layers of paper. Remember to cut two sets of legs. Cut the two slits at the bottom of the body and the slits at the top of the legs. Draw on black markings.

3 Slide the slits into each other.

SCARY SPIDER

It's a creepy-crawly spider.
You can make lots of big ones for
hanging at a Halloween party.

You will need
Black stiff paper
A compass, or a
plate and a jar lid
Paper scraps
Pencil, scissors,
ruler

1 Draw a 20 cm
(8 in) circle on the
paper using a compass
or a plate. Cut it out.
Draw a smaller circle,
about 8 cm (3 in) inside.

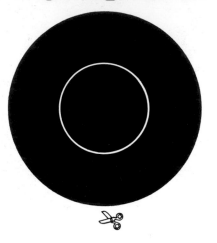

2 Draw eight double lines between
the circles for the legs. Cut away
the spaces shown in white.

3 Fold down the legs.
The creases are
about 1 cm (½ in) from
the body. Cut eyes from
paper scraps and glue
them on.

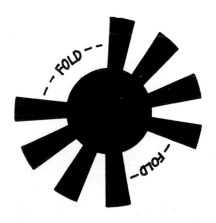

4   Scary Spider.

PET SHOW

Do you have a pet dog, cat or gerbil? Use them as models for making BIG cardboard stand-ups. If you don't have a pet, now you can have one as rare as a panda bear or as wild a kangaroo.

1 Draw a large picture of your pet on the card. Cut it out.

Other pets
Make other pet standups with cats, hamsters, ponies and anything else you like!

3 Pet Show.

2 Cut a long strip of card. Staple it into a circle. Staple or glue the animal to the circle.

Posters
Use pets made from large cards as stand-up posters to announce an after-school meeting or other information.

Napkin Rings
For fun table decorations, make smaller pets and staple them to smaller cardboard strips.

ANIMAL SKIN PAPERS

For an easy way to imitate animal skin markings you can sponge paper with paint. You can treat the paper before or after you make the animals.

You will need
White or brown paper
Poster paints
Sponge, scissors,
Disposable cups
Newspaper to protect
the working surface.

1 Cover your work surface with newspapers. Drop some paint in the bottom of a disposable cup. Mix in a few drops of water. The paint should remain fairly thick. Cut a small piece of sponge. Dip the sponge in the paint and dab it all over a piece of paper. Let it dry.

2 Animal Skin Paper.

Tiger Paper
Use yellow and brown paint. Let the first colour dry thoroughly before sponging on the second colour with a new piece of sponge.

Other animals
Imitate other animal skins, especially those with two contrasting colours. For example, small black and green dots for reptile paper. You could invent wild fantasy patterns in orange and purple. Use them not only to make animals, but also to make greeting cards.

SCALY ALLIGATOR

Alligators live in swampy warm waters. They are now an endangered species. Decorate posters with alligators and other endangered species to encourage people to preserve them.

You will need
A piece of paper
Scissors

1 Fold the paper in half lengthwise.

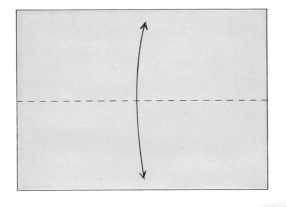

2 Draw an alligator. Use the folded edge for the back. Cut it out.

folded edge

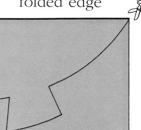

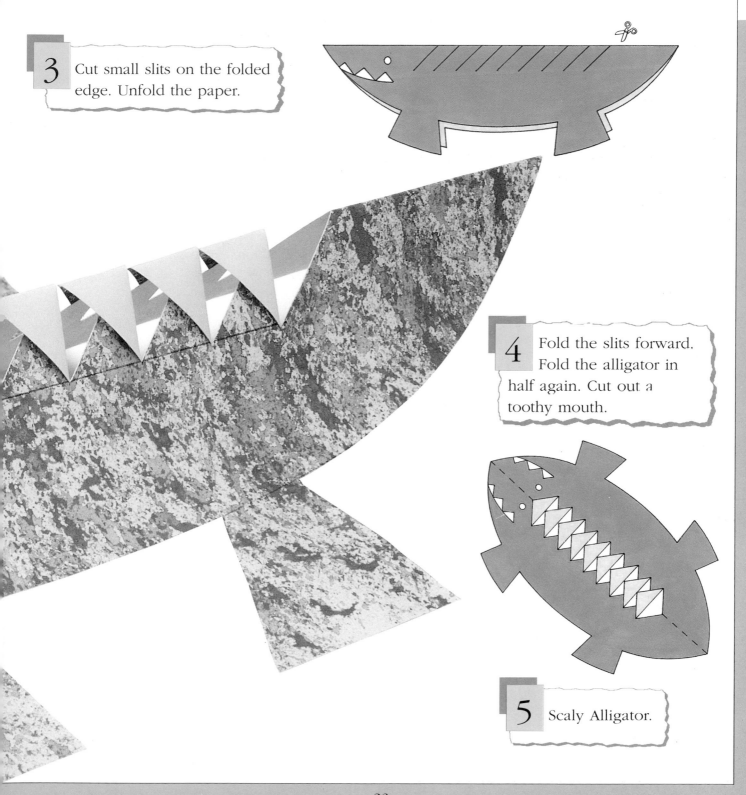

3 Cut small slits on the folded edge. Unfold the paper.

4 Fold the slits forward. Fold the alligator in half again. Cut out a toothy mouth.

5 Scaly Alligator.

UNICORN MASK

Unicorns are fantasy animals that are supposed to have the power to do good. Perhaps you'll have magic powers when you wear a unicorn mask.

You will need
Card
Pencil, scissors,
Felt-tip pens

1 Cut a large mask in the shape shown. Cut holes for eyes and nose.

2 Cut a long triangle. Fold it into three equal parts. Cut slits on the short edge. Bend the three tabs and paste the horn on the forehead of the mask.

3 Pierce holes on both sides of the mask. Tie on two pieces of string for tying around your head. Make two folds down the mask so that it bends around your face.

You can make all kinds of animal masks in the same way: elephants with long tusks, a dog with a long tongue and nose, or a rabbit with big teeth and floppy ears.

4 Unicorn mask.

BAT MOBILE

Bats are amazing creatures. They do not see very well, but fly in the dark using sonar (high-pitched sound waves and their echoes) to tell where things are.

You will need
Card
Pencil, scissors,
Felt-tip pens

1 Fold the square in half. Unfold. Fold in half the other way. Unfold. Turn the paper over.

2 Fold the square on the diagonal. Unfold, then fold the other diagonal. Do not unfold.

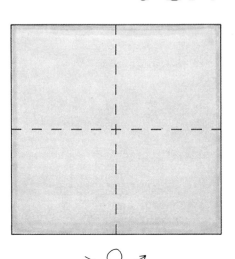

3 Hold the paper exactly as shown and gently push in until the paper overlaps and forms a double triangle.

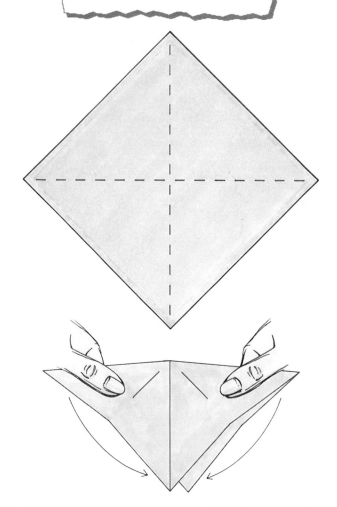

4 Fold the front flaps to the middle crease.

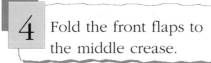

Helpful Hint
If you have trouble with step 3, you may not have turned over the paper in step 1. Go over the instructions again very carefully.

Bat Mobile
Make several bats. String them ready for hanging up.

5 Make small cuts where shown, on the back flaps.

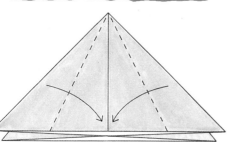

7 Bat.

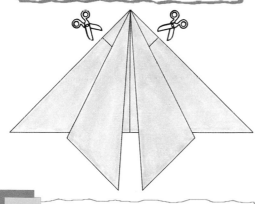

6 To make the head, fold the top forward at the cuts. Crease the wings forward lightly.

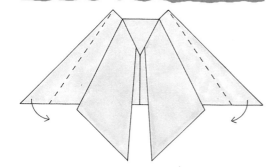

GOOGLY EYES

Googly Eyes is a fun animal or alien made by covering a ball of newspaper with papier mâché. You can decorate it in any wild way you like. The instructions show how to make the ball and then you are on your own.

You will need
Newspaper,
Wallpaper paste or PVC glue
(white glue),
Masking tape, kitchen foil,
Bowl, poster paint,
Felt-tip pens,
Paper scraps,
Scissors, pencil

1 Crunch a piece of newspaper into a ball. Cover it with masking tape to make it smoother.

2 Tear newspaper into strips. Soak them in a bowl with wallpaper paste or PVC glue diluted with a little water. Layer the strips in an overlapping pattern on the ball. You need about three layers. Set the ball on kitchen foil and let it dry for 24 hours.

3 Paint the ball. Glue on big eyes cut from black paper scraps and other weird things for antennae, or anything else you think the animal or alien might need.

Googly Eyes Animals
Try to make Googly Eyes look like a panda, a tiger, or any other animal.

BUTTERFLY

Everybody loves butterflies.
This one is pleated from wrapping
paper or magazine pages.

You will need
Giftwrap paper
20 cm (8 in) square
Giftwrap paper
10 cm (4 in) square
A wire twist or
pipecleaner

1 Fan pleat the large square
back and forth into 8 pleats.
Fan pleat the small square back
and forth into 4 pleats.

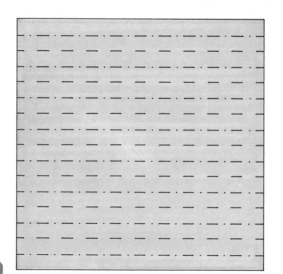

2 Tie the pleated squares together
in the middle with the wire twist
or pipecleaner (which makes the
butterfly's antennae). Stretch the
outside edges to spread the wings
apart. If they don't stay open, you
can glue any two edges to each
other close to the centre.

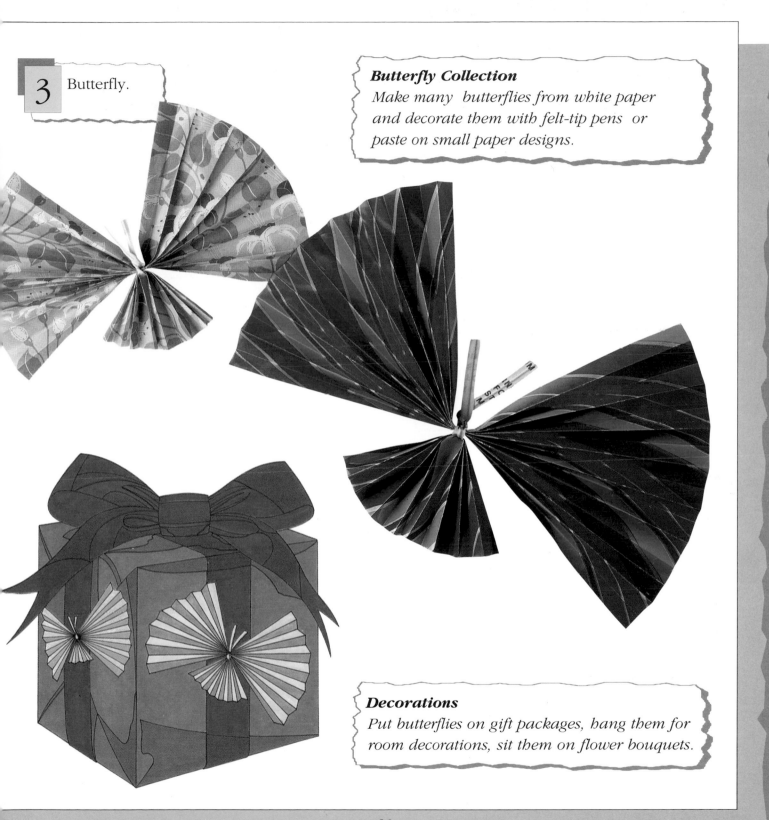

3 Butterfly.

Butterfly Collection
*Make many butterflies from white paper
and decorate them with felt-tip pens or
paste on small paper designs.*

Decorations
*Put butterflies on gift packages, hang them for
room decorations, sit them on flower bouquets.*

POISONOUS SNAKE

Make a scaly snake from two long strips of paper. It's an age-old paper trick that's called catstep. We don't know where the name came from, but people have folded catsteps for centuries. Once you have the hang of it, it's very, very simple. The strips can be the same colour or two different ones.

You will need
2 long strips of paper, 3 cm (1 in) wide
Scrap paper
Glue, scissors

1 Place the end of one strip over the other, at a right angle. Glue them together.

2 Fold the strip that is underneath over the top strip. Keep on folding the bottom strip over the top strip until the paper is used up.

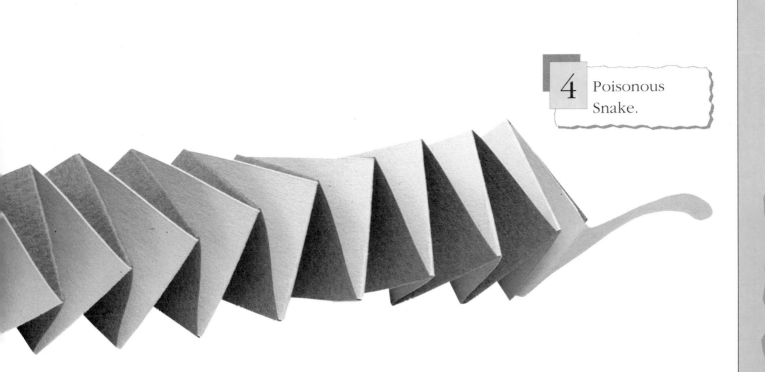

3 From scraps of paper cut a snake head and a snake tail. Glue them to each end of the snake. Add a mean, forked red tongue.

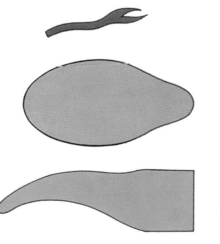

Garlands
Decorate large rooms or the Christmas tree with snake garlands made from wide strips of paper.

ORIGAMI PIG

You can fold paper squares into many different kinds of farm animal. The instructions show how you can make a pig.

You will need
A paper square

1 Fold the square in half. Unfold the paper and lie it flat. Then fold the top and bottom edges to the crease.

3 Unfold the four corners. Then hide them in between the main layers of paper, folding on the creases you just made. (In origami this is called a reverse fold.)

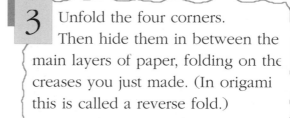

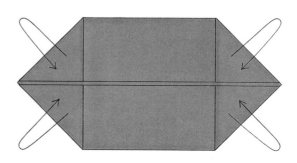

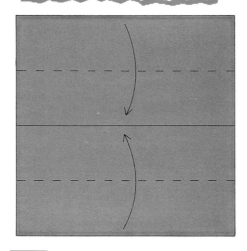

2 Fold all four corners to the middle.

4 Flip over two corners.

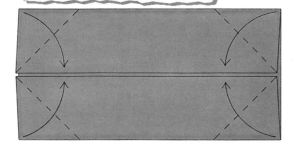

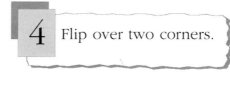

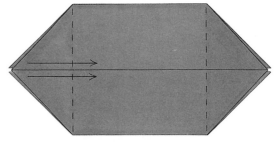

5 Fold the paper in half to the BACK.

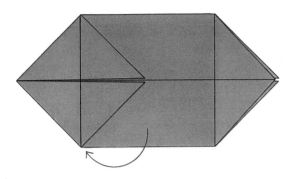

6 Make the legs. Fold the two corners on the front as shown. Repeat it with the two corners on the back.

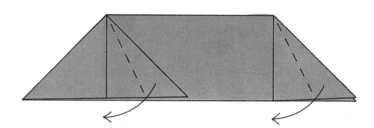

7 Fold the nose inside. Twist up the tail.

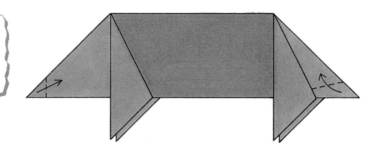

8 Origami Pig.

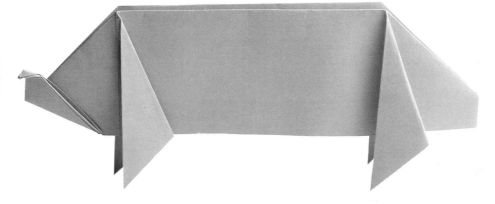

FIGHTING TURTLES

When you have ten minutes with nothing to do, play a game of Fighting Turtles with a friend. Cut two turtles from heavy paper. Set them on a table and bang your hand behind them. They will move as though they are fighting.

You will need
Heavy paper
Poncil, scissors

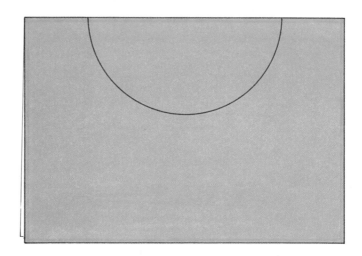

1 Fold the paper in half. Draw on half a circle, touching the folded edge.

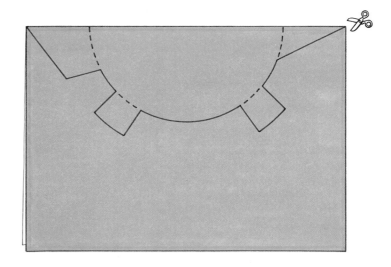

2 Add lines for the head, feet and tail. Cut on the outline.

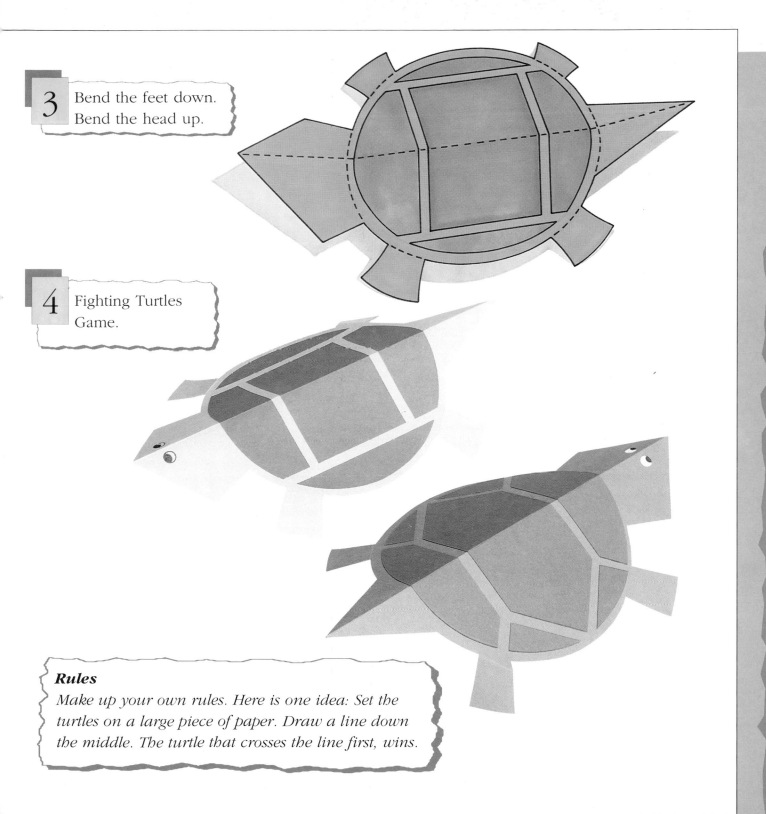

3 Bend the feet down. Bend the head up.

4 Fighting Turtles Game.

Rules

Make up your own rules. Here is one idea: Set the turtles on a large piece of paper. Draw a line down the middle. The turtle that crosses the line first, wins.

HUMMINGBIRD

Hummingbirds are friendly creatures that are attracted by anything red. Nature created them in many colours, which you can show on a greeting card.

You will need
A blank greeting card
Brightly-coloured paper
Tracing paper or photocopy
Glitter,
Felt-tip pens
Pencil, scissors, glue

1 Copy the outlines of the hummingbird and the smaller body.

2 Place the paper with the hummingbird outline on the purple paper. Staple both layers together outside the picture. Cut out through both layers.

3 Place the body outline on the pink paper. Staple both layers together. Cut out through both layers. Glue the body on the hummingbird. Draw in an eye. Glue the hummingbird on the blank greeting card.

4 Hummingbird Greeting Card.

Glitter

Imitate a hummingbird's iridescent feathers by spreading glue thinly on the tail and sprinkling on glitter.

ANIMAL MATCH-UP TOY

Have you ever seen a monkey with long, rabbit's ears? With this toy you'll see not only this weird monkey but lots of other weird and wonderful animals. You need a plate and a jar lid to draw two circles or you can use a compass instead.

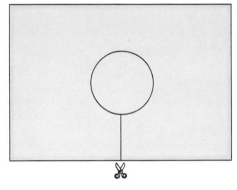

1 On a piece of paper draw a 20 cm (8 in) circle around the plate. Cut it out.

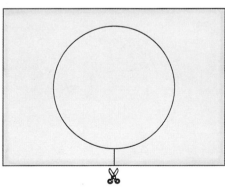

2 On another piece of paper draw a 11 cm (4½ in) circle around the jar lid. Cut it out.

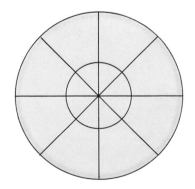

3 Poke a hole in the middle of both circles. Push the paper fastener through both circles. With pencil divide both circles into eight pie-shaped sections.

4 On another piece of paper draw eight animals 7 cm (3 in) tall. Draw the animals with long, narrow necks. Cut through the middle of the necks and glue the heads onto the small circle, and the bodies onto the large circle as shown.

5 This completes the Animal Match-Up Toy.

How to work your toy

Move the smaller circle around. You can match the head of each animal with its own body. Or you can make dozens of strange animals. How about a panda with a kangaroo baby pouch? Or a cat with spider legs?

DIORAMAS

Different animals live in different places. Some wild animals live in the African savannah. Domestic animals live on farms. Reptiles, and other animals that need very little water, have adapted to survive in the desert. And in a zoo, you can visit them all.

These different environments may be recreated in three-dimensional scenes, called dioramas. Find pictures of other animals and birds in books or magazines to help you construct them.

You could create an African Wildlife Park, including the zebra and giraffe on page 17. You could design other animals in the same way.

Or build a farm and include the dog (page 20) and the pig (page 34). You can design cows, lambs and other farm animals in the same way.

Or perhaps you could make a desert scene with crocodiles, lizards, snakes and turtles.

MORE ANIMALS AND BIRDS

There are hundreds of animals that you can make – just let your imagination go!

Here are some animals that you can try to make on your own. Perhaps you can use the animal skin papers that you might have made from page 21.

When you see an unusual animal on the television or at the zoo, try to draw it, then see if you can make a model of it. Keep it simple at first, but make your animals bright and colourful.